MONSOON!

An Extreme Weather Season

Mary O'Mara

The Rosen Publishing Group's
PowerKids Press™
New York

Published in 2009 by The Rosen Publishing Group, Inc.
29 East 21st Street, New York, NY 10010

Book Design: Haley W. Harasymiw

Photo Credits: Cover, pp. 5, 11, 14–15, 16 © AFP/Getty Images; p. 8 © TAOLMOR/Shutterstock; pp. 12–13 © Dana Ward/Shutterstock; pp. 18–19 © Lebedinski Vladislav/Shutterstock; p. 21 © Jim Reed/Science Faction/Getty Images; p. 22 © Cynthia Burkhardt/Shutterstock; p. 23 © Vladimir Vitek/Shutterstock; p. 24 http://en.wikipedia.org/wiki/Image:Lion-tailed_Macaque_in_Bristol_Zoo.jpg; pp. 25, 28 © National Geographic/Getty Images; p. 26 http://en.wikipedia.org/wiki/Image:Azmonsoon.jpg; p. 29 courtesy of earthobservatory.nasa.gov; p. 29 (Sahara Desert) © Vojko Kavcic/Shutterstock.

Library of Congress Cataloging-in-Publication Data

O'Mara, Mary.
  Monsoon! : an extreme weather season / Mary O'Mara.
    p. cm. — (Real life readers)
  Includes index.
  ISBN: 978-1-4358-0159-2
  6-pack ISBN: 978-1-4358-0160-8
  ISBN 978-1-4358-2988-6 (library binding)
  1. Monsoons—Juvenile literature. I. Title.
  QC939.M7O43 2009
  551.51'84—dc22

                              2008037531

Manufactured in the United States of America

Contents

What Is a Monsoon?

A monsoon is a pattern of winds that change direction with the seasons. It's formed by a hot land mass and a cooler body of water. The sun heats land more quickly than it heats a large body of water. Air near the ground heats and rises. Cooler air from the water moves over the land and takes its place. This action creates a constant wind. The moist air grows warmer, rises, cools again, and forms rain clouds. The clouds become heavy with moisture, and soon rain begins to fall. As long as winds continue to bring moist air over the land, the rain continues to fall.

The most famous monsoons blow over the northern part of the Indian Ocean. These strong winds and the huge amounts of rain they bring greatly affect the country of India. In some areas, a monsoon can bring more than 40 feet (12 m) of water over 4 months!

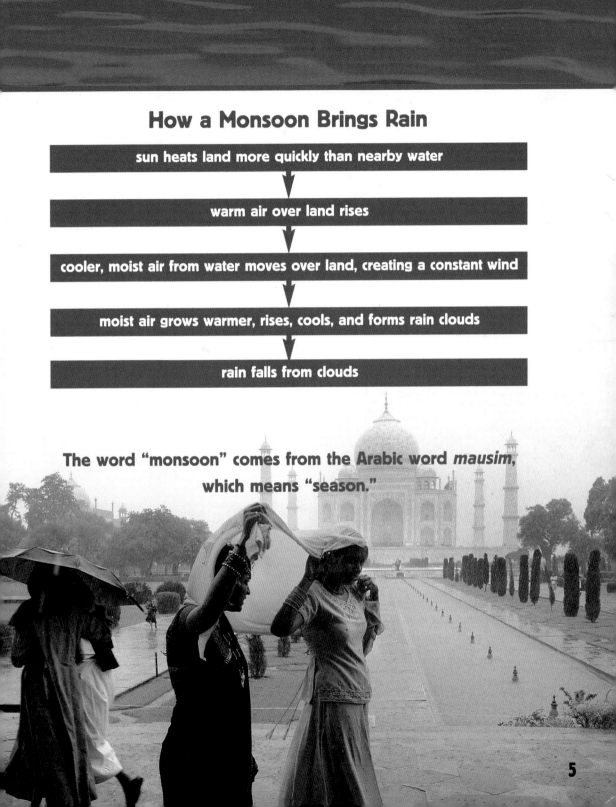

How a Monsoon Brings Rain

sun heats land more quickly than nearby water

warm air over land rises

cooler, moist air from water moves over land, creating a constant wind

moist air grows warmer, rises, cools, and forms rain clouds

rain falls from clouds

The word "monsoon" comes from the Arabic word *mausim,* which means "season."

India's Seasons

Weather in India is divided into three seasons. The hot season is from March to June. How hot is it? **Temperatures** in the Thar Desert can reach 123°F (51°C)! Other parts of the country get extremely hot as well. During this time, the air over the land rises as it grows warmer. The surrounding water remains cooler than the land.

The rainy, or monsoon, season lasts from about June to September. Monsoon winds blow the cool sea air from the southwest across the Arabian Sea, the northern part of the Indian Ocean. The moist air moves over the hot land and heats up. This air rises, cools, and makes thick, dark rain clouds. Soon, the clouds become heavy with moisture, and the rain begins. As long as the winds continue to blow in, the rain keeps falling. The greatest amounts of rain fall in northeastern India.

The Himalayas are huge mountains that stop monsoons from carrying rain to other parts of Asia.

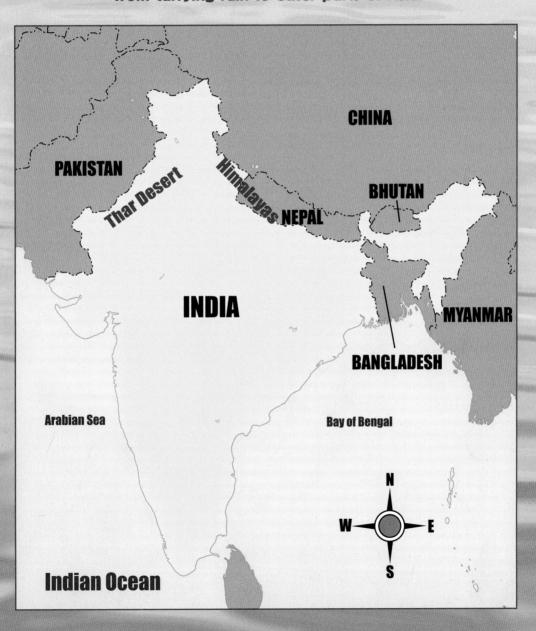

CHINA

PAKISTAN

Thar Desert

Himalayas

NEPAL

BHUTAN

INDIA

MYANMAR

BANGLADESH

Arabian Sea

Bay of Bengal

Indian Ocean

N
W   E
S

Most of the year, India is very dry. You can see in this picture that little grass grows in the hottest places.

The cool season in India lasts from about October to February. In most parts of the country, the days are cooler than they are in other months. Some places have freezing temperatures at night. Snow falls in the Himalayas. Cool air doesn't rise as warmer air does, so the moist winds from the water stop blowing inland. In fact, the winds change direction.

These dry winds blow from the northeast and mostly out over the Arabian Sea. However, some sweep over the Bay of Bengal and carry rain to other parts of India, but not nearly as much as the southwest winds. Most parts of India have to wait several months for more rain. In fact, the southwest monsoons bring 80 percent of all the rain that India receives in a year!

The Three Seasons of India

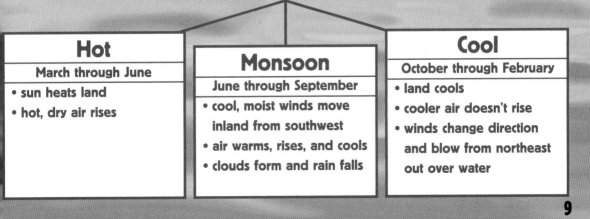

Hot	Monsoon	Cool
March through June	June through September	October through February
• sun heats land	• cool, moist winds move inland from southwest	• land cools
• hot, dry air rises	• air warms, rises, and cools	• cooler air doesn't rise
	• clouds form and rain falls	• winds change direction and blow from northeast out over water

How Much Does It Rain?

Do you wonder what it's like to live in India during the monsoon season? First, the winds bring very dark clouds—accompanied by thunder and lightning—over the land. From these clouds come heavy rains, which can last several days. People are so happy to see the first rainfall that some dance in the downpour! Many communities have special **festivals** to welcome the rain.

After the first stormy days, it may not rain all day long. Instead, it rains for a period of time every day for several days. The weather can change quickly during monsoon season. The sun may shine one minute followed by rain the next minute. It rains less and less as the season continues. However, rainfalls may continue to be very heavy even in September.

This elephant
was decorated
for a festival
welcoming the
monsoon rains
in India.

Monsoons and India's Farms

More than half of India's people are farmers, and farms cover about half the land. Most are small farms just big enough to grow food for the farmer's family. Some large farms grow food that's sold all over the world. Indian crops include cotton, corn, wheat, rice, and spices. India also grows most of the world's tea.

In this dry country, crops won't grow without the monsoon rains. Monsoon rainfall can also hurt India's farms. Too much rainfall washes away seeds and baby plants. If the rains come late, farmers must wait to plant seeds, and fewer crops are produced.

India has more cattle than any other country in the world. Cattle farmers need the monsoons to keep their animals and the plants they eat alive.

India needs the large amounts of food it grows. It has the second-largest population in the world.

If just a small amount of rain falls, farmers say that the monsoon "failed." Light rain won't make the soil wet enough to help grow healthy crops. If the monsoon doesn't bring any rain at all, **disasters** can occur. Long ago, no rain meant few crops. Few crops meant people didn't have enough to eat. In 1770, over 10 million Indian people died from hunger after a lack of monsoon rain.

Because India's large farms grow crops for other countries, a crop failure can mean higher food prices around the world. Today, food can be stored for use during bad crop years. Also, some farms use **irrigation systems** to supply their crops with water year round. However, most farmers growing food for their families cannot afford expensive tools or places to store food. These people still need the rain to come each year.

Even today, many of India's people are in danger of not having enough food or water when the rains don't come. This farmer waits for rain so he can grow rice.

Monsoons and India's Cities

Cities in India become very warm during the hot season. High populations and crowded conditions make the cities even hotter. Winds and rains from the Indian Ocean bring cooler weather. However, heavy rains can harm buildings and roads. Houses located in low places or near rivers flood easily.

Floods harm businesses as well. Many people sell their goods from carts and stands on the street. When the streets are flooded, they can't sell their goods, and people can't walk to buy from them.

Floods make drinking water unsafe since pollution can be washed into the water supply. Many illnesses travel through water as well. Floods kill almost 1,000 people in India each year.

Flooding can make life difficult in India's cities, as this picture shows. One town in India reported 30 feet (9 m) of rain in 1 month in 1861.

Mumbai (muhm-BY) was once a fishing village called Bombay. In the 1600s, British settlers arrived and helped build it into a major port. It's now the largest city in India, with almost 10 million people.

Because Mumbai is located on the coast of the Arabian Sea, it receives a lot of rain during monsoon season. Unfortunately, many people in Mumbai are very poor. About 1 million live in badly built shacks that can't withstand floodwaters and hard rain.

In 2006, the city recorded more than 37 inches (94 cm) of rain in 1 day! The rain continued the next day. Floods in the city

When the monsoon rains fall, sea levels rise and add to flood damage.

killed hundreds of people and left millions of others trapped. The government is looking for ways to send out flood warnings by radio, TV, and other forms of communication before dangerous monsoon weather occurs.

Forecasting the Monsoons

In the past, the people of India didn't know when the monsoons would arrive. In recent years, weather forecasters have begun to use computers and **satellites** to find where winds and rain clouds are forming. This allows them to collect and spread news more quickly.

During late April and early May, forecasters start looking for light winds beginning to blow from the southwest. Clouds then build up over southern India. This shows that the moist ocean air is moving over the land and rising to form clouds. Once the rain starts to fall, forecasters begin to track how fast the monsoon winds travel over the country.

Forecasters aren't always correct. They can't always tell how much rain will fall. However, weather forecasters often help farmers and other Indians **predict** when monsoons will arrive.

Satellite pictures use different colors to show different
amounts of rainfall.

Monsoons and India's Animals and Plants

The monsoons affect animals and plants in India, too. They flood the rivers, making sandy **riverbanks**. The next year, at the beginning of the hot season, female giant gharial (GEHR-ee-uhl) crocodiles of northern India dig holes in the sand. About 3 months later, the sands become very warm and cause baby gharial crocodiles to hatch. If the eggs don't hatch in time, they may wash away in a monsoon season flood.

The giant gharial crocodile can be 23 feet (7 m) long! It eats mostly fish,

Monsoon rains bring Indian elephants their food and water. Male elephants, called bulls, are larger than females, called cows. Males may be 10.5 feet (3.2 m) tall and weigh up to 8,000 pounds (3,632 kg). A male Indian elephant may eat about 300 pounds (136 kg) of food a day! Their food includes plants that need a lot of rain to grow, such as trees and grasses. Elephants can also need to drink up to 40 gallons (151 l) of water each day.

Indian
elephant

Many Indian plants have ways of storing water throughout the year. A monsoon forest is a special kind of **rain forest**. Trees in this forest lose their leaves during the hot season. This keeps water inside the trees. The leaves grow back when the monsoon season arrives, helping the trees make food.

The lion-tailed macaque (muh-KAK) is an animal that lives in India's forests. Like a lion, this kind of monkey has a face with a mane and a tail. Lion-tailed macaques live in

Only about 2,500 lion-tailed macaques remain in India today.

forests that receive up to 20 feet (6.1 m) of rain a year! The rain helps the trees grow the buds, fruits, and seeds that the macaques eat. These monkeys live only in India. Without the monsoons, they would disappear from Earth!

These trees show the great strength of the monsoon winds of India.

Nevada
Utah
Colorado
California
Arizona
New
Mexico
Texas
Gulf of California
MEXICO
Gulf
of
Mexico
Pacific
Ocean

These clouds announce the arrival of the monsoon season in Arizona.

Other Monsoons

Monsoons occur in other parts of the world, too. From about July to September, North America experiences monsoons. Wet air moves inland from the Gulf of Mexico, the Gulf of California, and the Pacific Ocean. Heavy rains fall on parts of Mexico and the southwestern United States. About 45 to 70 percent of the yearly rainfall in these desert areas occurs during this time. Mountains in southern California block the North American monsoons from traveling farther inland.

Monsoon rains supply North American desert plants and animals with water. However, just as in India, monsoons can cause harm, too. Heavy rains help more plants grow in the desert during the winter months than usual. The plants dry out in the summer heat and provide fuel for **wildfires**. Too little rain brings **drought** conditions and makes life much harder for farmers.

Monsoons affect Australia as well. From December to February, deserts in the middle of Australia reach their highest temperatures. This dry air rises and lets in the cooler air of the Indian Ocean. A season of strong winds and heavy rainfall lasts several months, mainly over northwestern Australia.

Parts of Africa also experience monsoon winds. From the end of June to October, cool winds from the Atlantic Ocean blow over lands near the Sahara Desert. Some scientists think two monsoons blow in during this period. One occurs in June and is mostly caused by the temperature differences between warm coastal waters and cooler ocean water. The second occurs in August and happens mainly because of the high temperature of the land.

monsoon clouds over Australia

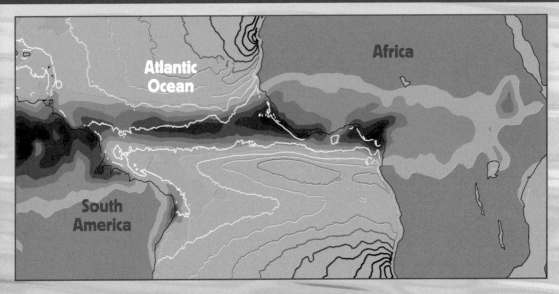

This map shows how the Atlantic Ocean carries moisture
to Africa, as well as South America, in June.
The yellow lines represent the warmest waters.

Sahara Desert

Monsoons: Feared and Loved

The monsoons of India and other parts of the world bring both harm and hope. Scientists continue to study these amazing weather patterns and try to figure out how to better forecast them. Each year, millions of people welcome both the beginning and end of the monsoon season.

India's Monsoon Rains	
too much rain	**too little rain**
• washes away seeds and small plants on farms • washes away gharial crocodile eggs • floods cities • can harm buildings and kill people	• crops won't grow • plants won't grow fruits and leaves for animals • people and animals can die from hunger

Glossary

disaster (dih-ZAS-tuhr) An event that causes suffering or loss.

drought (DROWT) A period of dryness that causes harm to crops.

festival (FEHS-tuh-vuhl) A day or special time of rejoicing or feasting.

irrigation system (ihr-uh-GAY-shun SIHS-tuhm) A method of carrying water to land through paths or pipes.

predict (prih-DIHKT) To say what will happen before it does.

rain forest (RAYN FOHR-uhst) A forest found in an area of heavy rainfall, usually located in the warmest areas of Earth.

riverbank (RIH-vuhr-bank) The land along the edge of a river.

satellite (SA-tuh-lyt) A machine that circles Earth and can be used to track weather.

temperature (tehm-pruh-chur) How hot or cold something is.

wildfire (WYLD-fyr) A fire that spreads quickly, especially in wilderness.

Index

Due to the changing nature of Internet links, The Rosen Publishing Group, Inc., has developed an online list of Web sites related to the subject of this book. This site is updated regularly. Please use this link to access the list: http://www.rcbmlinks.com/rlr/mons